NINJA FOODI GRILL COOKBOOK 2020

Healthy and Quick-to-Make Recipes for Indoor Grilling & Air Frying
that Anyone Can Cook

BY TONY LEE

CONTENTS

INTRODUCTION 7

CHAPTER 1: EVERYTHING YOU WANT TO KNOW ABOUT NINJA FOODI GRILL ...8

THE KING OF GRILLING 9

COOKING COMPONENTS 11

THE NINJA FOODI ADVANTAGE 13

TIPS AND SUGGESTIONS FOR COOKING PERFECTION 15

CHAPTER 2: BREAKFASTS 16

KALE SAUSAGE BREAKFAST 16

COCONUT BREAKFAST BAGELS 18

PINEAPPLE FRENCH TOAST 20

CREAMED FRENCH TOAST 22

CHAPTER 3: APPETIZERS & SNACKS 24

CRISPED BRUSSELS SPROUTS 24

CAJUNED EGGPLANT APPETIZER 26

HONEYED ASPARAGUS 27

GRILLED MAPLE BROCCOLI 29

POTATO CHIPS 31

GRILLED CHEESE PINEAPPLE 32

CHAPTER 4: CHICKEN & TURKEY **34**

CHICKEN ALFREDO APPLES 34

CLASSIC TURKEY BURGERS 36

GRILLED ORANGE CHICKEN 38

GRILLED BBQ TURKEY 40

CHICKEN TOMATINO 42

CHICKEN HOT BBQ 44

MOROCCAN ROASTED CHICKEN 46

CHICKEN BACON HAMBURGERS 48

ROSEMARY CHICKEN ROAST 50

ULTIMATE CHICKEN CRISPS 52

TURKEY TOMATO BURGERS 54

CHICKEN ZUCCHINI KEBABS 56

CHAPTER 5: PORK, BEEF & LAMB **58**

GRILLED BEEF BURGERS 58

ASIAN STYLE PORK RIBS 60

CLASSIC GARLIC GRILLED PORK CHOPS 62

HONEY GARLIC BEEF ROAST 64

RED WINE ROASTED BRISKET 66

SPICED STEAK POTATOES 68

HERBED LAMB CHOPS 70

HERB ROASTED BEEF 72

ASIAN STYLE APPLE STEAK 74

SHERRIED PORK ROAST 76

CRISPED PORK CHOPS 78

CHAPTER 6: FISH & SEAFOOD **80**

GRILLED SALMON BURGERS 80

GRILLED SALMON WITH CUCUMBER SAUCE 82

SHRIMP SKEWERS WITH YOGURT SAUCE 84

CRISPED SHRIMP WITH CHILI SAUCE 86

FISH GREENS BOWL 88

BBQ ROASTED SHRIMPS 90

ARUGULA SHRIMP 92

CRISPED FISH NUGGETS 94

GARLIC ROASTED SALMON 96

GRILLED SOY COD 98

CHAPTER 7: VEGETARIAN **100**

MUSTARD GREEN VEGGIES 100

CREAMY CORN POTATOES 102

VEGETABLE PASTA DELIGHT 104

APPLE GREEN SALAD 106

CHAPTER 8: DESSERTS **108**

GRILLED PINEAPPLE WITH ICE CREAM 108

CHOCO PECAN FUDGE 110

GORGEOUS GRILLED PEACHES 112

CONCLUSION **114**

INTRODUCTION

Backyard grilling is one of the most favorite summer activities to devour charred cuisines. These days you can find a kitchen appliance for anything, from slow cookers to multi-cookers. We know that you love grilling; however, no one wants their home filled with smoke and then consume sub-par grilled food. But what if you can enjoy all of your favorite grilled meals with ease and without much hassle with just one cooking unit.

Ninja Foodi Grill has been invented with the aim of providing an easy and convenient indoor grilling experience with cooking perfection. Apart from grilling, you can Air Fry, Roast, Bake, and Dehydrate using the technological marvel.

Ninja Foodi grill uses cyclonic high-temperature air to grill, air fry, roast, and bake a wide range of recipes. This versatile equipment provides the perfect combination of safety, convenience, and flavor-rich grilled meals.

You do not need to be an expert chef to learn to operate the Ninja Foodi grill; this kitchen appliance comes with easy to operate grilling functions supported by utmost safety features. This book perfectly suits beginners with a dedicated chapter to know everything about this amazing indoor grilling unit.

Explore the whole new world of perfectly char-grilled recipes with this exclusive Ninja Foodi Grill cookbook. From sizzling steak and roasted meats to BBQ shrimps and grilled salmon, Ninja Foodi Grill is your go-to equipment to replicate your favorite backyard grilled recipes with indoor grilled recipes. This cookbook acts as an all-in-one guide to know everything about the Ninja Grill to fulfill your desire to prepare healthy and flavor-rich indoor grilled cuisines.

Impress your guests over block parties and get-to-gather with juicy burgers and mouth-watering barbeque meats. This cookbook covers 50 Ninja Foodi Grill recipes divided into exclusive chapters of breakfasts, appetizers, snacks, chicken and poultry, pork, beef and lamb, fish and seafood, vegetarian, and desserts.

Be ready to learn the secret of perfectly indoor grilled meals. Welcome to the exciting world of Ninja Foodi Grill!

CHAPTER 1: EVERYTHING YOU WANT TO KNOW ABOUT NINJA FOODI GRILL

We all love grilled and roasted meals. People are increasingly consuming restaurant grilled foods, while it may be a convenient option, but it does come with many lifestyle hazards such as high blood pressure, obesity, high cholesterol, high blood sugar, and high sodium levels.

When you prepare your favorite foods at home, it gives you a great advantage of control over ingredients. Restaurant foods are high with sodium, sugar, saturated fats, cholesterol, and bad carbohydrates. With Ninja Foodi Grill, you can prepare the healthy grill, air fried and roasted recipes by controlling the amount of salt, sugar, and fat to your preference.

Ninja Foodi Grill is a versatile indoor grill unit providing 5-in-1 cooking functions to prepare your favorite grilled foods. Bring alive your BBQ parties with perfectly grilled cuisines. It offers intuitive designs with easy to operate functions to custom grill your favorite recipes. Its intuitive programmed settings, you can adjust time and temperature to grill foods to your satisfaction.

Ninja Foodi 5-in-one model comes with 6-quart cooking pot, ceramic coated grill, a pack of 5 kebab skewers, a cleaning brush, and 4-quart crisping basket.

The King of Grilling

Your investment and trust in this fantastic grilling unit reward you with lots of smiles and happy memories. If you are wondering why Ninja Foodi Grill and not any other appliance, then here is your answer.

GRILLING

Ninja Foodi uses high-temperature cyclonic air that allows you to cook recipes in just a matter of a few minutes. This cyclonic air reaches 500°F to enable superfast grilling to create caramelized char and juiciness.

The unit provides various options to grill as per your preferences and requirements. Different foods require different grill setting to caramelize and create the necessary level of juiciness. Ninja Foodi provides 4 grilling settings from Low to Max.

Low – This setting is mostly used for grilling softer ingredients such as sausage, vegetables, and bacon.

Medium – Most recipes use this setting as it creates an ideal grilling temperature to cook marinated meats, fish, seafood, and many vegetable recipes.

High – This setting is mostly used for foods requiring high-temperature grillings, such as burger patties, steaks, and chicken. However, many such recipes also use a Medium setting.

Max – This setting is used less frequently; it suits best to grill frozen foods, a few seafood ingredients, and some vegetables and fruits.

ROASTING

Roasting is done for many chickens, meat, fish, seafood, and vegetable recipes. Apart from main course meals, you can also prepare appetizers and sides using this setting.

AIR CRISP

This setting needs no introduction, as you can guess its use. Prepare all of your favorite crunchy foods using this setting. This setting requires you to use a crisping basket. Mostly used to prepare appetizers, sides, crunchy snacks, chicken nuggets, chicken wings, and some vegetable recipes.

BAKING

Ninja Foodi Grill also provides an additional feature of baking that coverts the unit into an oven. You can directly add the food inside the cooking pot or can use a multipurpose pan. Select this function and set your time to bake recipes just like a traditional oven.

DEHYDRATING

Dehydrate herbs, meats, fruits, and vegetables using the setting. Ninja Foodi Grill saves you from purchasing a separate dehydrator by providing this inbuilt dehydrating function.

Cooking Components

Cooking Pot

The preinstalled cooking pot is ceramic coated. A grilling plate is inserted over this pot to begin the cooking process. For other recipes, food ingredients can be directly added to this pot.

Crisping Basket

As the name suggests, the crisping basket is used to prepare crispy, tender recipes. You can adjust all of your crispy favorites using this basket with the AIR CRISP function. The basket is ceramic coated and also used for preparing dehydrated recipes using the DEHYDRATE function.

Hood

Hood comes with a fan that circulates air to caramelize inside food ingredients evenly. It also ensures that the smoke and flavor remain inside for the best cooking results.

Grease Collector

Ninja Foodi generates grease during the cooking process. Located behind the Ninja Foodi unit, the grease collector ensures that all the grease remains inside and does not spill over your kitchen platform.

Grilling Grate

Grilling grate holds the added ingredients and gets heated up to 500°F during the cooking process. With the use of evenly circulated cyclonic air, it ensures that the added food is grilled on one side and gets evenly seared.

Splatter Protection/Shield

A splatter protective shield lies between the hood and the cooking pot. As the name suggests, it prevents smoking and ensures that the heating element remains clean.

The Ninja Foodi Advantage

- A house party or a get-to-gather event involves many guests. But your favorite grilled foods are not only for them. With Ninja Foodi, you can prepare meals in smaller quantities in real quick time. Unlike outdoor grilling, you don't have to invest time in preparing things. Just press a few buttons and enjoy perfectly char-grilled recipes whenever you want.

- Weather changes during winter and monsoon can spoil your plans for outdoor grilling. With indoor grilling convenience, you do not have to worry about weather changes and can prepare recipes whenever the mood strikes. Moreover, the thermostat and rheostat ensure constant high internal temperature for even grilling.

- Outdoor grilling involves dealing with flames, smokes, and inflammable fluids, which then calls for some prior experience. If you are new to grilling and worrying about safety then Ninja Foodi is your answer. Equipped with high standard, latest safety features, this marvelous unit ensures utmost safety without the risk of burn injuries. The unit is entirely insulated and protected with outside layers for a totally safe cooking experience. During cooking, if the internal temperature rises beyond safety level, then the unit automatically shuts down to reduce temperature to a safe point.

- High-temperature cyclonic air circulates the food inside Ninja Foodi, and that is why many recipes do not require flipping during cooking time. Your food gets cooked evenly from top to bottom.

- Unlike outdoor grilling, cleaning Ninja Foodi after you are done with cooking is a breeze. Without leaving any soot, it cooks tender and flavorful recipes so that you only require to clean the grilling plates and unit with a dry or slightly damp cloth piece. Grill plates are ceramic-coated and nonstick for easy cleaning. Moreover, it's cooking pot, crisping basket, grill plates, skewers, and other accessories are totally dishwasher safe.

- Ninja Foodi is compact in design that demands a tiny space in your kitchen. As it does not involve multiple cooking utensils, you can quickly unwind and store it in any compact storage area.

- Despite being an indoor electric grill, Ninja Foodi does not add heavily to your electricity bill. It is an energy-efficient unit that consumes minimal power for economical cooking.

Tips and Suggestions for Cooking Perfection

- Avoid over-crowding the pot as it creates an unwanted obstruction to prevent the ideal circulation of high-temperature cyclonic air. Such obstruction impacts the quality of grilled recipes as well as baked, roasted, and air-fry recipes too. You might end up with partially cooked or one side cooked meals. When adding ingredients over the grille plate, cooking pot, or crisping basket, ensure some space between the elements such as chicken wings, chicken breasts, pork chops, steak ribs, lamb chops, turkey breasts, fish fillets, shrimps, etc.

- Preheating highly recommended as it creates an ideal warmth to start the cooking process. It takes about 5-8 minutes for the unit to preheat and signals a beeping sound to signal its readiness.

- Use wooden or silicone utensils to add and flip the ingredients to prevent scratching.

- Clean the components such as grilling plates, skewers, crisping basket, etc. before the next use. Accumulated oil and other particles affect the flavor and quality.

- Although this book covers all of your favorite recipes but if you want to prepare any other favorite recipes that used traditional grilling, then you can easily convert them for Ninja Foodi Grill. Reduce the recipe temperature to 25°F and cook for the same time to produce the same quality and flavor.

- If you want to prepare foods in large quantity, then the best way is to make in small batches instead of jamming Ninja Foodi. Due to 4-6 quart capacity, prepare food in batches for the best results.

Kale Sausage Breakfast

Prep Time: 5-10 min.

Cooking Time: 10 min.

Number of Servings: 4

Ingredients:

1 medium sweet yellow onion

4 medium eggs

4 sausage links

2 cups kale, chopped

1 cup mushrooms

Olive oil as required

Directions:

1. Take Ninja Foodi Grill, arrange it over your kitchen platform, and open the top lid.
2. Arrange the grill grate and close the top lid.
3. Press "GRILL" and select the "HIGH" grill function. Adjust the timer to 5 minutes and then press "START/STOP." Ninja Foodi will start pre-heating.
4. Ninja Foodi is preheated and ready to cook when it starts to beep. After you hear a beep, open the top lid.
5. Arrange the sausages over the grill grate.
6. Close the top lid and cook for 2 minutes. Now open the top lid, flip the sausages.
7. Close the top lid and cook for three more minutes.
8. Take out the grilled sausages.
9. Take a multi-purpose pan and lightly grease it with some cooking oil. Spread the onion, mushrooms, and kale; add the grilled sausages and crack the eggs in between the sausages.
10. Open the lid and arrange the pan directly inside the pot.
11. Press "BAKE" and adjust the temperature to 350°F. Adjust the timer to 5 minutes and then press "START/STOP."
12. Close the top lid and allow it to cook until the timer reads zero.
13. Serve warm.

Nutritional Values (Per Serving):

Calories: 236
Fat: 12g
Saturated Fat: 2g
Trans Fat: 0g
Carbohydrates: 17g
Fiber: 4g
Sodium: 369mg
Protein: 18g

Coconut Breakfast Bagels

Prep Time: 5-10 min.

Cooking Time: 8 min.

Number of Servings: 4

Ingredients:

1 cup fine sugar

2 tablespoons black coffee, prepared and cooled down

4 bagels, halved

1/4 cup coconut milk

2 tablespoons coconut flakes

Directions:

1. Take Ninja Foodi Grill, arrange it over your kitchen platform, and open the top lid.
2. Arrange the grill grate and close the top lid.
3. Press "GRILL" and select the "MED" grill function. Adjust the timer to 4 minutes and then press "START/STOP." Ninja Foodi will start pre-heating.
4. Ninja Foodi is preheated and ready to cook when it starts to beep. After you hear a beep, open the top lid.
5. Arrange 2 bagels over the grill grate.
6. Close the top lid and cook for 2 minutes. Now open the top lid, flip the bagels.
7. Close the top lid and cook for 2 more minutes.
8. Allow cooking until the timer reads zero. Divide into serving plates.
9. Grill the remaining bagels in a similar way. In a mixing bowl, whisk the remaining ingredients.
10. Serve the grilled bagels with the prepared sauce on top.

Nutritional Values (Per Serving):

Calories: 395
Fat: 23g
Saturated Fat: 12g
Trans Fat: 0g
Carbohydrates: 42.5g
Fiber: 4g
Sodium: 358mg
Protein: 18.5g

Pineapple French Toast

Prep Time: 5-10 min.

Cooking Time: 15 min.

Number of Servings: 4-5

Ingredients:

10 bread slices

1/4 cup sugar

1/4 cup milk

3 large eggs

1 cup coconut milk

10 slices pineapple (1/4-inch-thick), peeled

1/2 cup coconut flakes

Cooking spray

Directions:

1. In a mixing bowl, whisk the coconut milk, sugar, eggs, and milk. Dip the bread in this mixture and set aside for about 2 minutes.
2. Take Ninja Foodi Grill, arrange it over your kitchen platform, and open the top lid.
3. Arrange the grill grate and close the top lid.
4. Press "GRILL" and select the "MED" grill function. Adjust the timer to 4 minutes and then press "START/STOP." Ninja Foodi will start pre-heating.
5. Ninja Foodi is preheated and ready to cook when it starts to beep. After you hear a beep, open the top lid.
6. Arrange half the bread slices over the grill grate.
7. Close the top lid and cook for 2 minutes. Now open the top lid, flip the slices.
8. Close the top lid and cook for 2 more minutes.
9. Allow cooking until the timer reads zero. Divide into serving plates.
10. Repeat with the remaining slices. And then grill the pineapple slices with the same amount of time (flipping after 2 minutes).
11. Serve warm with the grilled bread topped with some coconut flakes.

Nutritional Values (Per Serving):

Calories: 202
Fat: 15g
Saturated Fat: 4g
Trans Fat: 0g
Carbohydrates: 49g
Fiber: 3g
Sodium: 214mg
Protein: 8g

Creamed French Toast

Prep Time: 5-10 min.

Cooking Time: 4 min.

Number of Servings: 2-3

Ingredients:

Juice of ½ orange

3 slices challah bread

2 medium eggs

½ quart strawberries, quartered

1 tablespoon balsamic vinegar

1/4 cup heavy cream

1 tablespoon honey

1 teaspoon orange zest

½ teaspoon vanilla extract

1/2 sprig rosemary

Salt to taste

Directions:

1. Take a foil sheet and add the strawberries, balsamic vinegar, orange juice, rosemary, and zest. Fold edges to create a pocket.
2. In a mixing bowl, whisk the egg; add the cream, honey, vanilla, and a pinch of salt and whisk again.
3. Dip the bread slices to coat evenly in the mixture.
4. Take Ninja Foodi Grill, arrange it over your kitchen platform, and open the top lid.
5. Arrange the grill grate and close the top lid.
6. Press "GRILL" and select the "MED" grill function. Adjust the timer to 4 minutes and then press "START/STOP." Ninja Foodi will start pre-heating.
7. Ninja Foodi is preheated and ready to cook when it starts to beep. After you hear a beep, open the top lid.

8. Arrange the foil packet and bread slices over the grill grate.
9. Close the top lid and cook for 2 minutes. Now open the top lid, flip the flip.
10. Close the top lid and cook for 2 more minutes.
11. Allow cooking until the timer reads zero. Divide into serving plates.
12. Serve warm the bread with the strawberry mixture.

Nutritional Values (Per Serving):

Calories: 369
Fat: 11.5g
Saturated Fat: 5g
Trans Fat: 0g
Carbohydrates: 36g
Fiber: 3.5g
Sodium: 186mg
Protein: 15g

Crisped Brussels Sprouts

Prep Time: 5-10 min.

Cooking Time: 12 min.

Number of Servings: 4

Ingredients:

1 pound Brussels sprouts, halved

2 tablespoons olive oil, extra-virgin

½ teaspoon ground black pepper

1 teaspoon sea salt

6 slices bacon, chopped

Directions:

1. In a mixing bowl, toss the Brussels sprouts, olive oil, salt, black pepper, and bacon.
2. Take Ninja Foodi Grill, arrange it over your kitchen platform, and open the top lid.
3. Arrange the Crisping Basket inside the pot.
4. Press "AIR CRISP" and adjust the temperature to 390°F. Adjust the timer to 12 minutes and then press "START/STOP." Ninja Foodi will start pre-heating.
5. Ninja Foodi is preheated and ready to cook when it starts to beep. After you hear a beep, open the top lid.
6. Arrange the Brussels sprout mixture directly inside the basket.
7. Close the top lid and cook for 6 minutes. After 6 minutes, shake the basket and close the top lid and cook for another 6 minutes.
8. Serve warm.

Nutritional Values (Per Serving):

Calories: 279
Fat: 18.5g
Saturated Fat: 4g
Trans Fat: 0g
Carbohydrates: 12.5g
Fiber: 4g
Sodium: 874mg
Protein: 14.5g

Cajuned Eggplant Appetizer

Prep Time: 5-10 min.

Cooking Time: 10 min.

Number of Servings: 4

Ingredients:

2 tablespoons lime juice

3 teaspoons Cajun seasoning

2 small eggplants, cut into slices (1/2 inch)

1/4 cup olive oil

Directions:

1. Coat the eggplant slices with the oil, lemon juice, and Cajun seasoning.
2. Take Ninja Foodi Grill, arrange it over your kitchen platform, and open the top lid.
3. Arrange the grill grate and close the top lid.
4. Press "GRILL" and select the "MED" grill function. Adjust the timer to 10 minutes and then press "START/STOP." Ninja Foodi will start pre-heating.
5. Ninja Foodi is preheated and ready to cook when it starts to beep. After you hear a beep, open the top lid.
6. Arrange the eggplant slices over the grill grate.
7. Close the top lid and cook for 5 minutes. Now open the top lid, flip the eggplant slices.
8. Close the top lid and cook for 5 more minutes.
9. Divide into serving plates.
10. Serve warm.

Nutritional Values (Per Serving):

Calories: 362
Fat: 11g
Saturated Fat: 3g
Trans Fat: 0g
Carbohydrates: 16g
Fiber: 1g
Sodium: 694mg
Protein: 8g

Honeyed Asparagus

Prep Time: 5-10 min.

Cooking Time: 15 min.

Number of Servings: 4

Ingredients:

2 pound asparagus, trimmed

1/2 teaspoon pepper

1 teaspoon salt

1/4 cup honey

2 tablespoons olive oil

4 tablespoons tarragon, minced

Directions:

1. Combine the asparagus with oil, salt, pepper, honey, and tarragon. Toss well.
2. Take Ninja Foodi Grill, arrange it over your kitchen platform, and open the top lid.
3. Arrange the grill grate and close the top lid.
4. Press "GRILL" and select the "MED" grill function. Adjust the timer to 8 minutes and then press "START/STOP." Ninja Foodi will start pre-heating.
5. Ninja Foodi is preheated and ready to cook when it starts to beep. After you hear a beep, open the top lid.
6. Arrange the asparagus over the grill grate.
7. Close the top lid and cook for 4 minutes. Now open the top lid, flip the asparagus.
8. Close the top lid and cook for 4 more minutes.
9. Serve warm.

Nutritional Values (Per Serving):

Calories: 241
Fat: 15g
Saturated Fat: 3g
Trans Fat: 0g
Carbohydrates: 31g
Fiber: 1g
Sodium: 103mg
Protein: 7.5g

Grilled Maple Broccoli

Prep Time: 5-10 min.

Cooking Time: 10 min.

Number of Servings: 4

Ingredients:

2 heads broccoli, cut into florets

4 tablespoons soy sauce

2 tablespoons canola oil

4 tablespoons balsamic vinegar

2 teaspoons maple syrup

Red pepper flakes and sesame seeds to garnish

Directions:

1. In a mixing bowl, add the soy sauce, balsamic vinegar, oil, and maple syrup. Whisk well and add the broccoli; toss well.
2. Take Ninja Foodi Grill, arrange it over your kitchen platform, and open the top lid.
3. Arrange the grill grate and close the top lid.
4. Press "GRILL" and select the "MAX" grill function. Adjust the timer to 10 minutes and then press "START/STOP." Ninja Foodi will start pre-heating.
5. Ninja Foodi is preheated and ready to cook when it starts to beep. After you hear a beep, open the top lid.
6. Arrange the broccoli over the grill grate.
7. Close the top lid and allow to cook until the timer reads zero.
8. Divide into serving plates.
9. Serve warm with red pepper flakes and sesame seeds on top.

Nutritional Values (Per Serving):

Calories: 141

Fat: 7g

Saturated Fat: 1g

Trans Fat: 0g

Carbohydrates: 14g

Fiber: 4g

Sodium: 853mg

Protein: 4.5g

Potato Chips

Prep Time: 5-10 min.

Cooking Time: 8-10 hours

Number of Servings: 2-3

Ingredients:

1 sweet potato, peeled and cut into slices

½ teaspoon sea salt

½ tablespoon avocado oil

Directions:

1. In a mixing bowl, toss the slice, and oil until evenly coated. Season with the salt to taste.
2. Take Ninja Foodi Grill, arrange it over your kitchen platform, and open the top lid.
3. Arrange the Crisping Basket inside the pot.
4. Press "DEHYDRATE" and adjust the temperature to 120°F. Adjust the timer to 8 hours and then press "START/STOP." Ninja Foodi will start pre-heating.
5. Ninja Foodi is preheated and ready to cook when it starts to beep. After you hear a beep, open the top lid.
6. Arrange the slices in a single layer directly inside the basket.
7. Close the top lid and allow it to cook until the timer reads zero. Dehydrate for 2 more hours if the slices are not crisp enough.
8. Serve warm.

Nutritional Values (Per Serving):

Calories: 146
Fat: 5g
Saturated Fat: 1g
Trans Fat: 0g
Carbohydrates: 22.5g
Fiber: 2g
Sodium: 651mg
Protein: 2g

Grilled Cheese Pineapple

Prep Time: 5-10 min.

Cooking Time: 8 min.

Number of Servings: 4

Ingredients:

Pineapple:

1 pineapple

3 tablespoons honey

2 tablespoons lime juice

1/4 cup packed brown sugar

Dip:

3 ounces cream cheese, softened

1 tablespoon brown sugar

1 tablespoon lime juice

2 tablespoons honey

1/4 cup yogurt

1 teaspoon grated lime zest

Directions:

1. Make 8 wedges from the pineapple and divide each wedge into 2 spears.
2. In a mixing bowl, combine the spears with the sugar, lime juice, and honey; refrigerate for 1 hour.
3. Combine all the dip ingredients in another bowl and set aside.
4. Remove the pineapple spears from the bowl.
5. Take Ninja Foodi Grill, arrange it over your kitchen platform, and open the top lid.
6. Arrange the grill grate and close the top lid.
7. Press "GRILL" and select the "MED" grill function. Adjust the timer to 8 minutes and then press "START/STOP." Ninja Foodi will start pre-heating.

8. Ninja Foodi is preheated and ready to cook when it starts to beep. After you hear a beep, open the top lid.
9. Arrange the spears over the grill grate.
10. Close the top lid and cook for 4 minutes. Now open the top lid, flip the spears.
11. Close the top lid and cook for 4 more minutes.
12. Divide into serving plates.
13. Serve warm with the prepared dip.

Nutritional Values (Per Serving):

Calories: 328
Fat: 6g
Saturated Fat: 1.5g
Trans Fat: 0g
Carbohydrates: 48.5g
Fiber: 8g
Sodium: 98mg
Protein: 7g

Chicken Alfredo Apples

Prep Time: 5-10 min.

Cooking Time: 20 min.

Number of Servings: 4

Ingredients:

1 large apple, wedged

1 tablespoon lemon juice

4 chicken breasts, halved

4 teaspoons chicken seasoning

4 slices provolone cheese

1/4 cup blue cheese, crumbled

1/2 cup Alfredo sauce

Directions:

1. Season the chicken in a bowl with chicken seasoning. In another bowl, toss the apple with lemon juice.
2. Take Ninja Foodi Grill, arrange it over your kitchen platform, and open the top lid.
3. Arrange the grill grate and close the top lid.
4. Press "GRILL" and select the "MED" grill function. Adjust the timer to 16 minutes and then press "START/STOP." Ninja Foodi will start pre-heating.
5. Ninja Foodi is preheated and ready to cook when it starts to beep. After you hear a beep, open the top lid.
6. Arrange the chicken over the grill grate.
7. Close the top lid and cook for 8 minutes. Now open the top lid, flip the chicken.
8. Close the top lid and cook for 8 more minutes.
9. Then after, grill the apple in the same manner for 2 minutes per side.
10. Serve the chicken with the apple, blue cheese, and alfredo sauce.

Nutritional Values (Per Serving):

Calories: 247
Fat: 19g
Saturated Fat: 3g
Trans Fat: 0g
Carbohydrates: 29.5g
Fiber: 2g
Sodium: 853mg
Protein: 14.5g

Classic Turkey Burgers

Prep Time: 5-10 min.

Cooking Time: 12 min.

Number of Servings: 4

Ingredients:

1 jalapeño pepper, seeded, stemmed, and minced

3 tablespoons bread crumbs

1 pound turkey, ground

½ red onion, minced

½ teaspoon cayenne pepper

1 ½ teaspoons ground cumin

1 teaspoon paprika

½ teaspoon sea salt

½ teaspoon ground black pepper

4 burger buns

Optional to include - Lettuce, tomato, cheese, and ketchup and mustard

Directions:

1. In a large mixing bowl, add the ground turkey, red onion, jalapeño pepper, bread crumbs, cumin, paprika, cayenne pepper, salt, and black pepper. Combine the mixture well.
2. Prepare four patties from the mixture.
3. Take Ninja Foodi Grill, arrange it over your kitchen platform, and open the top lid.
4. Arrange the grill grate and close the top lid.
5. Press "GRILL" and select the "MED" grill function. Adjust the timer to 12 minutes and then press "START/STOP." Ninja Foodi will start pre-heating.

6. Ninja Foodi is preheated and ready to cook when it starts to beep. After you hear a beep, open the top lid.
7. Arrange the patties over the grill grate.
8. Close the top lid and allow it to cook until timer reads zero.
9. Arrange the buns and place the patties over them. Add your choice of toppings: lettuce, tomato, cheese, ketchup, and/ or mustard. Serve fresh.

Nutritional Values (Per Serving):

Calories: 301
Fat: 13.5g
Saturated Fat: 3g
Trans Fat: 0g
Carbohydrates: 28.5g
Fiber: 3g
Sodium: 561mg
Protein: 25.5g

Grilled Orange Chicken

Prep Time: 5-10 min.

Cooking Time: 10 min.

Number of Servings: 5-6

Ingredients:

2 teaspoons ground coriander

1/2 teaspoon garlic salt

1/4 teaspoon ground black pepper

12 chicken wings

1 tablespoon canola oil

Sauce:

1/4 cup butter, melted

3 tablespoons honey

1/2 cup orange juice

1/3 cup Sriracha chili sauce

2 tablespoons lime juice

1/4 cup chopped cilantro

Directions:

1. Coat the chicken with the oil and season with the spices; refrigerate for 2 hours to marinate.
2. Combine all the sauce ingredients and set aside. Optionally, you can stir-cook the sauce mixture for 3-4 minutes in a saucepan.
3. Take Ninja Foodi Grill, arrange it over your kitchen platform, and open the top lid.
4. Arrange the grill grate and close the top lid.

5. Press "GRILL" and select the "MED" grill function. Adjust the timer to 10 minutes and then press "START/STOP." Ninja Foodi will start pre-heating.
6. Ninja Foodi is preheated and ready to cook when it starts to beep. After you hear a beep, open the top lid.
7. Arrange the chicken over the grill grate.
8. Close the top lid and cook for 5 minutes. Now open the top lid, flip the chicken.
9. Close the top lid and cook for 5 more minutes.
10. Serve warm with the prepared sauce on top.

Nutritional Values (Per Serving):

Calories: 327
Fat: 14g
Saturated Fat: 3.5g
Trans Fat: 0g
Carbohydrates: 19g
Fiber: 1g
Sodium: 258mg
Protein: 25g

Grilled BBQ Turkey

Prep Time: 5-10 min.

Cooking Time: 30 min.

Number of Servings: 5-6

Ingredients:

1/2 cup minced parsley

1/2 cup chopped green onions

4 garlic cloves, minced

1 cup Greek yogurt

1/2 cup lemon juice

1 teaspoon dried rosemary, crushed

1/3 cup canola oil

4 tablespoons minced dill

1 teaspoon salt

1/2 teaspoon pepper

1-3 pound turkey breast half, bone in

Directions:

1. In a mixing bowl, combine all the ingredients except the turkey. Add and coat the turkey evenly. Refrigerate for 8 hours to marinate.
2. Take Ninja Foodi Grill, arrange it over your kitchen platform, and open the top lid.
3. Arrange the grill grate and close the top lid.
4. Press "GRILL" and select the "HIGH" grill function. Adjust the timer to 30 minutes and then press "START/STOP." Ninja Foodi will start pre-heating.
5. Ninja Foodi is preheated and ready to cook when it starts to beep. After you hear a beep, open the top lid.
6. Arrange the turkey over the grill grate.
7. Close the top lid and cook for 15 minutes. Now open the top lid, flip the turkey.

8. Close the top lid and cook for 15 more minutes. Cook until the food thermometer reaches 350°F.
9. Slice and serve.

Nutritional Values (Per Serving):

Calories: 426
Fat: 8.5g
Saturated Fat: 2g
Trans Fat: 0g
Carbohydrates: 22g
Fiber: 3g
Sodium: 594mg
Protein: 38g

Chicken Tomatino

Prep Time: 5-10 min.

Cooking Time: 12 min.

Number of Servings: 4

Ingredients:

4 chicken breast, boneless and skinless

1/4 cup fresh basil leaves

8 plum tomatoes

3/4 cup vinegar

2 tablespoons olive oil

1 garlic clove, minced

1/2 teaspoon salt

Directions:

1. Take food processor or blender, open the lid and inside add the basil, vinegar, olive oil, salt, and garlic.
2. Blend to make a smooth mixture. Add the tomatoes and blend them again.
3. In a mixing bowl, add the chicken and tomato mixture. Combine the ingredients to mix well with each other.
4. Refrigerate for 1-2 hours to marinate.
5. Take Ninja Foodi Grill, arrange it over your kitchen platform, and open the top lid.
6. Arrange the grill grate and close the top lid.
7. Press "GRILL" and select the "HIGH" grill function. Adjust the timer to 6 minutes and then press "START/STOP." Ninja Foodi will start pre-heating.
8. Ninja Foodi is preheated and ready to cook when it starts to beep. After you hear a beep, open the top lid.
9. Arrange the chicken over the grill grate.
10. Close the top lid and cook for 3 minutes. Now open the top lid, flip the chicken.
11. Close the top lid and cook for 3 more minutes — Cook in batches in required.
12. Serve warm.

Nutritional Values (Per Serving):

Calories: 421
Fat: 6.5g
Saturated Fat: 3g
Trans Fat: 0g
Carbohydrates: 18g
Fiber: 3g
Sodium: 236mg
Protein: 23g

Chicken Hot BBQ

Prep Time: 5-10 min.

Cooking Time: 18 min.

Number of Servings: 4

Ingredients:

2 tablespoons honey

1 pound chicken drumsticks

1 tablespoon hot sauce

2 cups barbecue sauce

Juice of 1 lime

Ground black pepper and sea salt to taste

Directions:

1. In a mixing bowl, add the barbecue sauce, lime juice, honey, pepper, salt, and hot sauce. Combine and set aside.
2. In a mixing bowl, add the ½ cup of the sauce and chicken. Combine the ingredients to mix well with each other.
3. Refrigerate for 1 hour to marinate.
4. Take Ninja Foodi Grill, arrange it over your kitchen platform, and open the top lid.
5. Arrange the grill grate and close the top lid.
6. Press "GRILL" and select the "MED" grill function. Adjust the timer to 18 minutes and then press "START/STOP." Ninja Foodi will start pre-heating.
7. Ninja Foodi is preheated and ready to cook when it starts to beep. After you hear a beep, open the top lid.
8. Arrange the chicken over the grill grate.
9. Close the top lid and allow to cook until the timer reads zero. Cook until the food thermometer reaches 165°F.
10. Serve warm.

Nutritional Values (Per Serving):

Calories: 423
Fat: 13.5g
Saturated Fat: 4g
Trans Fat: 0g
Carbohydrates: 47.5g
Fiber: 4g
Sodium: 1148mg
Protein: 22g

Moroccan Roasted Chicken

Prep Time: 5-10 min.

Cooking Time: 22 min.

Number of Servings: 4

Ingredients:

3 tablespoons plain yogurt

4 skinless, boneless chicken thighs

4 garlic cloves, chopped

½ teaspoon Kosher salt

1/3 cup olive oil

1/2 cup fresh flat-leaf parsley, finely chopped

2 teaspoons ground cumin

2 teaspoons paprika

1/4 teaspoon crushed red pepper flakes

Directions:

1. Take food processor or blender, open the lid and inside add the garlic, yogurt, salt, and oil.
2. Blend to make a smooth mixture. Refrigerate the mixture.
3. In a mixing bowl, add the chicken, red pepper flakes, paprika, cumin, parsley, and garlic. Combine the ingredients to mix well with each other.
4. Refrigerate for 2-4 hours to marinate.
5. Take Ninja Foodi Grill, arrange it over your kitchen platform, and open the top lid. Lightly grease cooking pot with some oil or cooking spray.
6. Press "ROAST" and adjust the temperature to 400°F. Adjust the timer to 23 minutes and then press "START/STOP." Ninja Foodi will start pre-heating.
7. Ninja Foodi is preheated and ready to cook when it starts to beep. After you hear a beep, open the top lid.
8. Arrange the chicken directly inside the pot.
9. Close the top lid and cook for 15 minutes. Now open the top lid, flip the chicken.
10. Close the top lid and cook for 8 more minutes.
11. Serve warm with the yogurt dip.

Nutritional Values (Per Serving):

Calories: 321
Fat: 24.5g
Saturated Fat: 5g
Trans Fat: 0g
Carbohydrates: 6g
Fiber: 1g
Sodium: 602mg
Protein: 21g

Chicken Bacon Hamburgers

Prep Time: 5-10 min.

Cooking Time: 25 min.

Number of Servings: 4

Ingredients:

1 tablespoon honey

4 chicken breasts, halves

1/4 cup mayonnaise

1 tablespoon Dijon mustard

1/2 teaspoon Montreal seasoning

4 hamburger buns, split

2 bacon strips, cooked and crumbled

4 slices Swiss cheese

Lettuce leaves and tomato slices, optional

Directions:

1. Pound the chicken into ½ inch thickness. Season it with the seasoning and set aside.
2. Take Ninja Foodi Grill, arrange it over your kitchen platform, and open the top lid.
3. Arrange the grill grate and close the top lid.
4. Press "GRILL" and select the "MED" grill function. Adjust the timer to 12 minutes and then press "START/STOP." Ninja Foodi will start pre-heating.
5. Ninja Foodi is preheated and ready to cook when it starts to beep. After you hear a beep, open the top lid.
6. Arrange the chicken over the grill grate.
7. Close the top lid and cook for 6 minutes. Now open the top lid, flip the chicken.
8. Close the top lid and cook for 6 more minutes.
9. In a mixing bowl, mix the mayonnaise with honey and mustard.
10. Arrange the buns and place the chicken over them; add the mayo mixture on top. Add your choice of toppings: 1 cheese slices, bacon, and other toppings.
11. Serve fresh.

Nutritional Values (Per Serving):

Calories: 293
Fat: 23.5g
Saturated Fat: 4g
Trans Fat: 0g
Carbohydrates: 36g
Fiber: 3g
Sodium: 482mg
Protein: 26g

Rosemary Chicken Roast

Prep Time: 5-10 min.

Cooking Time: 35 min.

Number of Servings: 4

Ingredients:

1 lemon

2-pounds whole rotisserie chicken

3 garlic cloves, minced

½ teaspoon salt

1 teaspoon ground pepper

1 sprig rosemary

1 tablespoon sage

Directions:

1. Squeeze half the lemon and rub the lemon juice all over the chicken. Season with some salt and pepper. Add the rosemary, sage, garlic cloves, and sliced lemon inside the chicken cavity.
2. Take Ninja Foodi Grill, arrange it over your kitchen platform, and open the top lid. Lightly grease cooking pot with some oil or cooking spray.
3. Press "ROAST" and adjust the temperature to 350°F. Adjust the timer to 30 minutes and then press "START/STOP." Ninja Foodi will start pre-heating.
4. Ninja Foodi is preheated and ready to cook when it starts to beep. After you hear a beep, open the top lid.
5. Arrange the chicken directly inside the pot. Slice half the lemon and arrange them in circles around the chicken.
6. Close the top lid and allow to cook until the timer reads zero. Cook until the food thermometer reaches 350°F.
7. Serve warm.

Nutritional Values (Per Serving):

Calories: 456
Fat: 33g
Saturated Fat: 8.5g
Trans Fat: 0g
Carbohydrates: 5g
Fiber: 0.5g
Sodium: 469mg
Protein: 42g

Ultimate Chicken Crisps

Prep Time: 5-10 min.

Cooking Time: 11 min.

Number of Servings: 2

Ingredients:

⅛ cup bread crumbs

¼ teaspoon sea salt

¼ teaspoon black pepper, freshly ground

½ pound boneless and skinless chicken breasts, cut into cutlets

½ tablespoon extra-virgin olive oil

¼ teaspoon garlic powder

¼ teaspoon paprika

⅛ teaspoon onion powder

Directions:

1. Evenly coat the chicken cutlets with the oil.
2. In a mixing bowl, add the bread crumbs, salt, pepper, paprika, garlic powder, and onion powder. Combine the ingredients to mix well with each other.
3. Add the chicken and coat well.
4. Take Ninja Foodi Grill, arrange it over your kitchen platform, and open the top lid.
5. Arrange the Crisping Basket inside the pot.
6. Press "AIR CRISP" and adjust the temperature to 375°F. Adjust the timer to 9 minutes and then press "START/STOP." Ninja Foodi will start pre-heating.
7. Ninja Foodi is preheated and ready to cook when it starts to beep. After you hear a beep, open the top lid.
8. Arrange the chicken directly inside the basket.
9. Close the top lid and allow to cook until the timer reads zero. Cook until the food thermometer reaches 165°F.
10. Serve warm.

Nutritional Values (Per Serving):

Calories: 203
Fat: 7.5g
Saturated Fat: 1g
Trans Fat: 0g
Carbohydrates: 6.5g
Fiber: 1g
Sodium: 358mg
Protein: 26g

Turkey Tomato Burgers

Prep Time: 5-10 min.

Cooking Time: 40 min.

Number of Servings: 6

Ingredients:

2/3 cup sun-dried tomatoes, chopped

1/4 teaspoon salt

1/4 teaspoon pepper

1 large red onion, chopped

1 cup crumbled feta cheese

2 pounds lean ground turkey

6 burger buns of your choice, sliced in half

Directions:

1. In a mixing bowl, add all the ingredients. Combine the ingredients to mix well with each other.
2. Prepare six patties from the mixture.
3. Take Ninja Foodi Grill, arrange it over your kitchen platform, and open the top lid.
4. Arrange the grill grate and close the top lid.
5. Press "GRILL" and select the "MED" grill function. Adjust the timer to 14 minutes and then press "START/STOP." Ninja Foodi will start pre-heating.
6. Ninja Foodi is preheated and ready to cook when it starts to beep. After you hear a beep, open the top lid.
7. Arrange the patties over the grill grate.
8. Close the top lid and cook for 7 minutes. Now open the top lid, flip the patties.
9. Close the top lid and cook for 7 more minutes.
10. Serve warm with ciabatta rolls. Add your choice of toppings: lettuce, tomato, cheese, ketchup, cheese, etc.

Nutritional Values (Per Serving):

Calories: 298
Fat: 16g
Saturated Fat: 2.5g
Trans Fat: 0g
Carbohydrates: 32g
Fiber: 4g
Sodium: 321mg
Protein: 27.5g

Chicken Zucchini Kebabs

Prep Time: 5-10 min.

Cooking Time: 15 min.

Number of Servings: 4

Ingredients:

Juice of 4 lemons

Grated zest of 1 lemon

1 pound boneless, skinless chicken breasts, cut into cubes of 2 inches

2 tablespoons plain Greek yogurt

¼ cup extra-virgin olive oil

4 garlic cloves, minced

1 teaspoon sea salt

½ teaspoon ground black pepper

2 tablespoons dried oregano

1 red onion, quartered

1 zucchini, sliced

Directions:

1. In a mixing bowl, add the Greek yogurt, oil, lemon juice, zest, garlic, oregano, salt, and pepper. Combine the ingredients to mix well with each other.
2. Add the chicken and coat well. Refrigerate for 1-2 hours to marinate.
3. Take Ninja Foodi Grill, arrange it over your kitchen platform, and open the top lid.
4. Arrange the grill grate and close the top lid.
5. Press "GRILL" and select the "MED" grill function. Adjust the timer to 14 minutes and then press "START/STOP." Ninja Foodi will start pre-heating.
6. Take the skewers, thread the chicken, red onion, and zucchini. Thread alternatively.
7. Ninja Foodi is preheated and ready to cook when it starts to beep. After you hear a beep, open the top lid.

8. Arrange the skewers over the grill grate.
9. Close the top lid and allow it to cook until the timer reads zero. Baste the kebabs with a marinating mixture in between. Cook until the food thermometer reaches 165°F.
10. Serve warm.

Nutritional Values (Per Serving):

Calories: 277
Fat: 15.5g
Saturated Fat: 2g
Trans Fat: 0g
Carbohydrates: 9.5g
Fiber: 2g
Sodium: 523mg
Protein: 25g

Grilled Beef Burgers

Prep Time: 5-10 min.

Cooking Time: 10 min.

Number of Servings: 4

Ingredients:

4 ounces cream cheese

4 slices bacon, cooked and crumbled

2 seeded jalapeño peppers, stemmed, and minced

½ cup shredded Cheddar cheese

½ teaspoon chili powder

¼ teaspoon paprika

¼ teaspoon ground black pepper

2 pounds ground beef

4 hamburger buns

4 slices pepper Jack cheese

Optional - Lettuce, sliced tomato, and sliced red onion

Directions:

1. In a mixing bowl, combine the peppers, Cheddar cheese, cream cheese, and bacon until well combined.
2. Prepare the ground beef into 8 patties. Add the cheese mixture onto four of the patties; arrange a second patty on top of each to prepare four burgers. Press gently.
3. In another bowl, combine the chili powder, paprika, and pepper. Sprinkle the mixture onto the sides of the burgers.
4. Take Ninja Foodi Grill, arrange it over your kitchen platform, and open the top lid.

5. Arrange the grill grate and close the top lid.
6. Press "GRILL" and select the "HIGH" grill function. Adjust the timer to 4 minutes and then press "START/STOP." Ninja Foodi will start pre-heating.
7. Ninja Foodi is preheated and ready to cook when it starts to beep. After you hear a beep, open the top lid.
8. Arrange the burgers over the grill grate.
9. Close the top lid and allow it to cook until the timer reads zero. Cook for 3-4 more minutes, if needed.
10. Cook until the food thermometer reaches 145°F. Serve warm.
11. Serve warm with buns. Add your choice of toppings: pepper Jack cheese, lettuce, tomato, and red onion.

Nutritional Values (Per Serving):

Calories: 783
Fat: 38g
Saturated Fat: 16g
Trans Fat: 0g
Carbohydrates: 25g
Fiber: 3g
Sodium: 1259mg
Protein: 57.5g

Asian Style Pork Ribs

Prep Time: 5-10 min.

Cooking Time: 25 min.

Number of Servings: 2

Ingredients:

¼ cup hoisin sauce

¼ cup hoisin sauce

1 teaspoon garlic powder

1 teaspoon onion powder

¼ cup soy sauce

¼ cup apple cider vinegar

1-pound pork ribs

Directions:

1. In a mixing bowl, add all the ingredients. Combine the ingredients to mix well with each other.
2. Add the pork ribs and coat well. Refrigerate for 2-4 hours to marinate.
3. Take Ninja Foodi Grill, arrange it over your kitchen platform, and open the top lid.
4. Arrange the grill grate and close the top lid.
5. Press "GRILL" and select the "MED" grill function. Adjust the timer to 24 minutes and then press "START/STOP." Ninja Foodi will start pre-heating.
6. Ninja Foodi is preheated and ready to cook when it starts to beep. After you hear a beep, open the top lid.
7. Arrange the pork ribs over the grill grate.
8. Close the top lid and cook for 12 minutes. Now open the top lid, flip the ribs.
9. Close the top lid and cook for 12 more minutes.
10. Serve warm.

Nutritional Values (Per Serving):

Calories: 326
Fat: 9g
Saturated Fat: 3g
Trans Fat: 0g
Carbohydrates: 26.5g
Fiber: 5g
Sodium: 529mg
Protein: 27g

Classic Garlic Grilled Pork Chops

Prep Time: 5-10 min.

Cooking Time: 15 min.

Number of Servings: 2

Ingredients:

2 tablespoons minced garlic

½ teaspoon salt

1 tablespoon cumin seed

1 tablespoon cracked black pepper

1 tablespoon olive oil

2 pork chops

Directions:

1. In a mixing bowl, add all the ingredients. Combine the ingredients to mix well with each other.
2. Add the pork chops and combine them well. Refrigerate for 2-4 hours to marinate.
3. Take Ninja Foodi Grill, arrange it over your kitchen platform, and open the top lid.
4. Arrange the grill grate and close the top lid.
5. Press "GRILL" and select the "MED" grill function. Adjust the timer to 15 minutes and then press "START/STOP." Ninja Foodi will start pre-heating.
6. Ninja Foodi is preheated and ready to cook when it starts to beep. After you hear a beep, open the top lid.
7. Arrange the pork chops over the grill grate.
8. Close the top lid and cook for 8 minutes. Now open the top lid, flip the chops.
9. Close the top lid and cook for 7 more minutes.
10. Serve warm.

Nutritional Values (Per Serving):

Calories: 418
Fat: 24g
Saturated Fat: 6g
Trans Fat: 0g
Carbohydrates: 9g
Fiber: 2g
Sodium: 654mg
Protein: 41g

Honey Garlic Beef Roast

Prep Time: 5-10 min.

Cooking Time: 30 min.

Number of Servings: 5-6

Ingredients:

½ cup balsamic vinegar

2 tablespoons olive oil

2-pounds boneless roast beef

½ cup beef organic beef broth

1 tablespoon coconut aminos

1 tablespoon honey

1 tablespoon Worcestershire sauce

½ teaspoon red pepper flakes

4 cloves of garlic, minced

Directions:

1. In a mixing bowl, add all the ingredients. Combine the ingredients to mix well with each other.
2. Add the roast beef and combine well. Refrigerate for 2-4 hours to marinate.
3. Take Ninja Foodi Grill, arrange it over your kitchen platform, and open the top lid. Lightly grease cooking pot with some oil or cooking spray.
4. Press "ROAST" and adjust the temperature to 380°F. Adjust the timer to 20 minutes and then press "START/STOP." Ninja Foodi will start pre-heating.
5. Ninja Foodi is preheated and ready to cook when it starts to beep. After you hear a beep, open the top lid.
6. Arrange the beef directly inside the pot.
7. Close the top lid and cook for 10 minutes. Now open the top lid, flip the beef.
8. Close the top lid and cook for 10 more minutes.
9. Serve warm.

Nutritional Values (Per Serving):

Calories: 372
Fat: 13g
Saturated Fat: 5.5g
Trans Fat: 0g
Carbohydrates: 11g
Fiber: 1g
Sodium: 257mg
Protein: 39.5g

Red Wine Roasted Brisket

Prep Time: 5-10 min.

Cooking Time: 45 min.

Number of Servings: 4

Ingredients:

3/4 cup red wine vinegar

1 large onion, sliced thinly

10 garlic cloves, minced

1 bunch cilantro, chopped

3-pounds beef brisket

Directions:

1. Take food processor or blender, open the lid and inside add the garlic, cilantro, red wine, and onions.
2. Blend to make a smooth mixture.
3. Take a zip-lock bag, add the garlic mixture, salt, pepper, and brisket in it. Shake well and refrigerate for 2-4 hours to marinate.
4. Take Ninja Foodi Grill, arrange it over your kitchen platform, and open the top lid. Lightly grease cooking pot with some oil or cooking spray.
5. Press "ROAST" and adjust the temperature to 350°F. Adjust the timer to 45 minutes and then press "START/STOP." Ninja Foodi will start pre-heating.
6. Ninja Foodi is preheated and ready to cook when it starts to beep. After you hear a beep, open the top lid.
7. Arrange the brisket directly inside the pot.
8. Close the top lid and allow it to cook until the timer reads zero.
9. Serve warm.

Nutritional Values (Per Serving):

Calories: 462
Fat: 16g
Saturated Fat: 5g
Trans Fat: 0g
Carbohydrates: 6.5g
Fiber: 1g
Sodium: 238mg
Protein: 56g

Spiced Steak Potatoes

Prep Time: 5-10 min.

Cooking Time: 25 min.

Number of Servings: 1-2

Ingredients:

2 teaspoons steak seasoning

2 russet potatoes, scrubbed and sliced

1 sirloin steak

1 tablespoon avocado oil

Directions:

1. In a mixing bowl, add the oil and steak seasoning. Combine the ingredients to mix well with each other.
2. Add the steak and coat well.
3. Take Ninja Foodi Grill, arrange it over your kitchen platform, and open the top lid.
4. Arrange the grill grate and close the top lid.
5. Press "GRILL" and select the "MED" grill function. Adjust the timer to 24 minutes and then press "START/STOP." Ninja Foodi will start pre-heating.
6. Ninja Foodi is preheated and ready to cook when it starts to beep. After you hear a beep, open the top lid.
7. Arrange the potatoes and steak over the grill grate.
8. Close the top lid and cook for 12 minutes. Now open the top lid, flip the potatoes and steak.
9. Close the top lid and cook for 12 more minutes.
10. Serve warm.

Nutritional Values (Per Serving):

Calories: 521
Fat: 34g
Saturated Fat: 11g
Trans Fat: 0g
Carbohydrates: 22g
Fiber: 4g
Sodium: 1687mg
Protein: 38g

Herbed Lamb Chops

Prep Time: 5-10 min.

Cooking Time: 15 min.

Number of Servings: 2

Ingredients:

1 tablespoon rosemary, chopped

3 tablespoons extra-virgin olive oil

1 garlic clove, minced

½ rack lamb (4 bones)

Ground black pepper and salt to taste

Directions:

1. In a mixing bowl, add the oil, garlic, and rosemary. Combine the ingredients to mix well with each other.
2. Add the lamb, salt and pepper; coat well. Refrigerate for 2-4 hours to marinate.
3. Take Ninja Foodi Grill, arrange it over your kitchen platform, and open the top lid.
4. Arrange the grill grate and close the top lid.
5. Press "GRILL" and select the "HIGH" grill function. Adjust the timer to 12 minutes and then press "START/STOP." Ninja Foodi will start pre-heating.
6. Ninja Foodi is preheated and ready to cook when it starts to beep. After you hear a beep, open the top lid.
7. Arrange the lamb rack over the grill grate.
8. Close the top lid and cook for 6 minutes. Now open the top lid, flip the lamb.
9. Close the top lid and cook for 6 more minutes. Cook until the food thermometer reaches 145°F.
10. Serve warm.

Nutritional Values (Per Serving):

Calories: 362
Fat: 29.5g
Saturated Fat: 6.5g
Trans Fat: 0g
Carbohydrates: 2g
Fiber: 0.5g
Sodium: 328mg
Protein: 22g

Herb Roasted Beef

Prep Time: 5-10 min.

Cooking Time: 30 min.

Number of Servings: 4-6

Ingredients:

1 teaspoon basil

½ teaspoon thyme

2-pounds beef round roast

1 onion, sliced thinly

3 tablespoons olive oil

½ cup water

¼ teaspoon black pepper

1 teaspoon salt

Directions:

1. In a mixing bowl, add all the ingredients. Combine the ingredients to mix well with each other.
2. Add the roast and coat well. Set aside for 15-30 minutes.
3. Take Ninja Foodi Grill, arrange it over your kitchen platform, and open the top lid. Lightly grease cooking pot with some oil or cooking spray.
4. Press "ROAST" and adjust the temperature to 380°F. Adjust the timer to 20 minutes and then press "START/STOP." Ninja Foodi will start pre-heating.
5. Ninja Foodi is preheated and ready to cook when it starts to beep. After you hear a beep, open the top lid.
6. Arrange the roast directly inside the pot.
7. Close the top lid and cook for 10 minutes. Now open the top lid, flip the roast.
8. Close the top lid and cook for 10 more minutes.
9. Carve the roast and serve warm.

Nutritional Values (Per Serving):

Calories: 326
Fat: 13g
Saturated Fat: 3g
Trans Fat: 0g
Carbohydrates: 7g
Fiber: 1g
Sodium: 502mg
Protein: 46g

Asian Style Apple Steak

Prep Time: 5-10 min.

Cooking Time: 13 min.

Number of Servings: 4

Ingredients:

3 tablespoons sesame oil

3 tablespoons brown sugar

1 ½ pounds beef tips

4 garlic cloves, minced

½ apple, peeled and grated

⅓ cup soy sauce

1 teaspoon ground black pepper

Sea salt to taste

Directions:

1. In a mixing bowl, add the garlic, apple, sesame oil, sugar, soy sauce, pepper, and salt. Combine the ingredients to mix well with each other.
2. Add the beef and coat well. Refrigerate for 1-2 hours to marinate.
3. Take Ninja Foodi Grill, arrange it over your kitchen platform, and open the top lid.
4. Arrange the grill grate and close the top lid.
5. Press "GRILL" and select the "MED" grill function. Adjust the timer to 14 minutes and then press "START/STOP." Ninja Foodi will start pre-heating.
6. Ninja Foodi is preheated and ready to cook when it starts to beep. After you hear a beep, open the top lid.
7. Arrange the beef over the grill grate.
8. Close the top lid and allow to cook until the timer reads 11 minutes. Cook until the food thermometer reaches 145°F. If needed, cook for 3 more minutes.
9. Slice and serve warm.

Nutritional Values (Per Serving):

Calories: 517
Fat: 29g
Saturated Fat: 10.5g
Trans Fat: 0g
Carbohydrates: 16.5g
Fiber: 2g
Sodium: 1198mg
Protein: 36g

Sherried Pork Roast

Prep Time: 5-10 min.

Cooking Time: 45-50 min.

Number of Servings: 4

Ingredients:

1/4 cup dry sherry

3 tablespoons honey

2-pounds pork roast, trimmed

1/3 cup soy sauce

2 cloves of garlic, minced

½ teaspoon ground ginger

Directions:

1. In a mixing bowl, add all the ingredients. Combine the ingredients to mix well with each other.
2. Add the pork roast and combine it well. Refrigerate for 10-12 hours to marinate.
3. Take Ninja Foodi Grill, arrange it over your kitchen platform, and open the top lid. Lightly grease cooking pot with some oil or cooking spray.
4. Press "ROAST" and adjust the temperature to 400°F. Adjust the timer to 25 minutes and then press "START/STOP." Ninja Foodi will start pre-heating.
5. Ninja Foodi is preheated and ready to cook when it starts to beep. After you hear a beep, open the top lid.
6. Arrange the roast directly inside the pot.
7. Close the top lid and cook for 15 minutes. Now open the top lid, flip the roast.
8. Close the top lid and cook for 10 more minutes.
9. Serve warm.

Nutritional Values (Per Serving):

Calories: 524
Fat: 19g
Saturated Fat: 6g
Trans Fat: 0g
Carbohydrates: 20.5g
Fiber: 2g
Sodium: 851mg
Protein: 58g

Crisped Pork Chops

Prep Time: 5-10 min.

Cooking Time: 25 min.

Number of Servings: 4

Ingredients:

1 egg

¼ cup milk

4 bone-in pork chops

Salt and ground black pepper to taste

4 teaspoons paprika

½ teaspoon garlic powder

½ teaspoon cayenne pepper

½ teaspoon dry mustard

1 cup Panko breadcrumbs

Directions:

1. Season the pork tenderloin with some salt and black pepper.
2. In a mixing bowl, combine the milk and egg.
3. In another bowl, add the breadcrumbs, paprika, garlic powder, cayenne pepper, and mustard. Combine the ingredients to mix well with each other.
4. Coat the pork tenderloin first in the egg mixture and then with the breadcrumb mixture.
5. Take Ninja Foodi Grill, arrange it over your kitchen platform, and open the top lid.
6. Arrange the Crisping Basket inside the pot.
7. Press "AIR CRISP" and adjust the temperature to 400°F. Adjust the timer to 25 minutes and then press "START/STOP." Ninja Foodi will start pre-heating.
8. Ninja Foodi is preheated and ready to cook when it starts to beep. After you hear a beep, open the top lid.
9. Arrange the pork tenderloin directly inside the basket.
10. Close the top lid and allow it to cook until the timer reads zero.
11. Serve warm.

Nutritional Values (Per Serving):

Calories: 328
Fat: 13g
Saturated Fat: 4.5g
Trans Fat: 0g
Carbohydrates: 15g
Fiber: 3g
Sodium: 436mg
Protein: 38.5g

Grilled Salmon Burgers

Prep Time: 5-10 min.

Cooking Time: 20 min.

Number of Servings: 2-3

Ingredients:

1/2 tablespoon Dijon mustard

1 ½ tablespoons shallot, finely chopped

1 tablespoon cilantro, minced

½ pound skinless salmon fillets, cubed

1/4 teaspoon salt

1 ½ garlic cloves, minced

½ tablespoon grated lime zest

½ tablespoon soy sauce

½ tablespoon honey

1/8 teaspoon pepper

2 hamburger buns, slice into half

Directions:

1. In a mixing bowl, combine all the ingredients. Prepare 2 patties from the mixture.
2. Take Ninja Foodi Grill, arrange it over your kitchen platform, and open the top lid.
3. Arrange the grill grate and close the top lid.
4. Press "GRILL" and select the "MED" grill function. Adjust the timer to 10 minutes and then press "START/STOP." Ninja Foodi will start pre-heating.
5. Ninja Foodi is preheated and ready to cook when it starts to beep. After you hear a beep, open the top lid.
6. Arrange the patties over the grill grate.

7. Close the top lid and cook for 5 minutes. Now open the top lid, flip the patties.
8. Close the top lid and cook for 5 more minutes.
9. Serve warm with buns. Add your choice of toppings: lettuce, cheese, tomato, etc.

Nutritional Values (Per Serving):

Calories: 394
Fat: 20.5g
Saturated Fat: 4g
Trans Fat: 0g
Carbohydrates: 22g
Fiber: 3g
Sodium: 203mg
Protein: 24g

Grilled Salmon with Cucumber Sauce

Prep Time: 5-10 min.

Cooking Time: 8 min.

Number of Servings: 4

Ingredients:

½ tablespoon lime zest, grated

1 tablespoon olive oil

1/4 teaspoon salt

1 tablespoon rice vinegar

2 teaspoons sugar

1/8 cup lime juice

1 cucumber, peeled and chopped

1/6 cup cilantro, chopped

1 garlic clove, minced

½ tablespoon onion, finely chopped

1 teaspoon minced ginger root

1/4 teaspoon ground coriander

1/4 teaspoon ground pepper

Salmon:

5 (6 ounces) salmon fillets

1/2 tablespoon olive oil

1/6 cup gingerroot, minced

1/4 teaspoon freshly ground pepper

½ tablespoon lime juice

1/4 teaspoon salt

Directions:

1. Take food processor or blender, open the lid and inside add the ingredients from the lime zest to ground pepper.
2. Blend to make a smooth mixture.
3. Season the salmon fillets with the ginger, oil, salt, black pepper, and lime juice.
4. Take Ninja Foodi Grill, arrange it over your kitchen platform, and open the top lid.
5. Arrange the grill grate and close the top lid.
6. Press "GRILL" and select the "MED" grill function. Adjust the timer to 8 minutes and then press "START/STOP." Ninja Foodi will start pre-heating.
7. Ninja Foodi is preheated and ready to cook when it starts to beep. After you hear a beep, open the top lid.
8. Arrange the fillets over the grill grate.
9. Close the top lid and cook for 4 minutes. Now open the top lid, flip the fillets.
10. Close the top lid and cook for 4 more minutes.
11. Serve warm with the prepared sauce.

Nutritional Values (Per Serving):

Calories: 449
Fat: 19g
Saturated Fat: 8.5g
Trans Fat: 0g
Carbohydrates: 18g
Fiber: 2g
Sodium: 511mg
Protein: 32g

Shrimp Skewers with Yogurt Sauce

Prep Time: 5-10 min.

Cooking Time: 8 min.

Number of Servings: 4

Ingredients:

2/3 cup fresh arugula

1/3 cup lemon juice

1/4 cup yogurt

2 teaspoons milk

2 tablespoons olive oil

1 pound shrimp, peeled and deveined

2 green onions, sliced

1/2 teaspoon salt

1/4 teaspoon ground black pepper

1 teaspoon Dijon mustard

2 garlic cloves, minced

1/2 teaspoon grated lemon zest

1 teaspoon cider vinegar

1/2 teaspoon sugar

12 cherry tomatoes

Directions:

1. In a mixing bowl, season the shrimp with lemon juice, lemon zest, oil, and garlic. Set aside for 10-15 minutes.
2. Take food processor or blender, open the lid and inside add the arugula, yogurt, milk, green onion, sugar, vinegar, mustard, and ¼ teaspoon salt.
3. Blend to make a smooth mixture.

4. Take the skewers, thread the seasoned shrimp and tomatoes. Thread alternatively. Season the skewers with salt and black pepper.
5. Take Ninja Foodi Grill, arrange it over your kitchen platform, and open the top lid.
6. Arrange the grill grate and close the top lid.
7. Press "GRILL" and select the "MED" grill function. Adjust the timer to 4 minutes and then press "START/STOP." Ninja Foodi will start pre-heating.
8. Ninja Foodi is preheated and ready to cook when it starts to beep. After you hear a beep, open the top lid.
9. Arrange the skewers over the grill grate.
10. Close the top lid and cook for 2 minutes. Now open the top lid, flip the skewers.
11. Close the top lid and cook for 2 more minutes.
12. Serve with the prepared sauce.

Nutritional Values (Per Serving):

Calories: 334
Fat: 4g
Saturated Fat: 0.5g
Trans Fat: 0g
Carbohydrates: 28g
Fiber: 2.5g
Sodium: 547mg
Protein: 15.5g

Crisped Shrimp with Chili Sauce

Prep Time: 5-10 min.

Cooking Time: 15 min.

Number of Servings: 4

Ingredients:

2 large eggs

¼ cup panko bread crumbs

¾ cup coconut flakes, unsweetened

½ cup all-purpose flour

2 teaspoons ground black pepper

½ teaspoon sea salt

24 peeled, deveined shrimp

Chili sauce of your choice

Directions:

1. In a mixing bowl, add the flour, black pepper, and salt. Combine the ingredients to mix well with each other.
2. In another bowl, whisk the eggs. In another bowl, combine the coconut flakes and bread crumbs
3. Coat the shrimps with the flour mixture and then coat with the egg mixture. Lastly, coat with the coconut mixture.
4. Take Ninja Foodi Grill, arrange it over your kitchen platform, and open the top lid.
5. Arrange the Crisping Basket inside the pot. Coat it with some cooking spray.
6. Press "AIR CRISP" and adjust the temperature to 400°F. Adjust the timer to 7 minutes and then press "START/STOP." Ninja Foodi will start pre-heating.
7. Ninja Foodi is preheated and ready to cook when it starts to beep. After you hear a beep, open the top lid.
8. Arrange the shrimps directly inside the basket.
9. Close the top lid and allow it to cook until the timer reads zero. Cook in batches if needed.
10. Serve warm with chili sauce.

Nutritional Values (Per Serving):

Calories: 356
Fat: 13.5g
Saturated Fat: 8g
Trans Fat: 0g
Carbohydrates: 24.5g
Fiber: 4g
Sodium: 413mg
Protein: 31g

Fish Greens Bowl

Prep Time: 5-10 min.

Cooking Time: 6 min.

Number of Servings: 4

Ingredients:

6 tablespoons extra-virgin olive oil

1 ½ pounds tuna, cut into four strips

2 tablespoons rice wine vinegar

¼ teaspoon sea salt

½ teaspoon ground black pepper

2 tablespoons sesame oil

1 (10-ounce) bag baby greens

½ English cucumber, sliced

Directions:

1. In a mixing bowl, add the rice vinegar, ¼ teaspoon of salt, and ½ teaspoon of pepper. Combine the ingredients to mix well with each other.
2. Add the oil and combine again.
3. Season the fish with salt and pepper, and drizzle with the sesame oil.
4. Take Ninja Foodi Grill, arrange it over your kitchen platform, and open the top lid.
5. Arrange the grill grate and close the top lid.
6. Press "GRILL" and select the "MAX" grill function. Adjust the timer to 6 minutes and then press "START/STOP." Ninja Foodi will start pre-heating.
7. Ninja Foodi is preheated and ready to cook when it starts to beep. After you hear a beep, open the top lid.
8. Arrange the fish over the grill grate.
9. Close the top lid and allow to cook until the timer reads zero.
10. Serve warm with the baby greens, veggies, and vinaigrette on top.

Nutritional Values (Per Serving):

Calories: 418
Fat: 28g
Saturated Fat: 4.5g
Trans Fat: 0g
Carbohydrates: 6.5g
Fiber: 2g
Sodium: 208mg
Protein: 35g

BBQ Roasted Shrimps

Prep Time: 5-10 min.

Cooking Time: 7 min.

Number of Servings: 2

Ingredients:

3 tablespoons minced chipotles in adobo sauce

¼ teaspoon salt

1/4 cup barbecue sauce

Juice of 1/2 orange

½-pound large shrimps

Directions:

1. In a mixing bowl, add all the ingredients. Combine the ingredients to mix well with each other.
2. Set aside to marinate for 15 minutes.
3. Take Ninja Foodi Grill, arrange it over your kitchen platform, and open the top lid. Lightly grease cooking pot with some oil or cooking spray.
4. Press "ROAST" and adjust the temperature to 400°F. Adjust the timer to 7 minutes and then press "START/STOP." Ninja Foodi will start pre-heating.
5. Ninja Foodi is preheated and ready to cook when it starts to beep. After you hear a beep, open the top lid.
6. Arrange the shrimps directly inside the pot.
7. Close the top lid and allow it to cook until the timer reads zero.
8. Serve warm.

Nutritional Values (Per Serving):

Calories: 173
Fat: 2g
Saturated Fat: 0.5g
Trans Fat: 0g
Carbohydrates: 21g
Fiber: 2g
Sodium: 1143mg
Protein: 17.5g

Arugula Shrimp

Prep Time: 5-10 min.

Cooking Time: 12 min.

Number of Servings: 4

Ingredients:

1/2 cup parsley, minced

1/3 cup pistachios, shelled

2 tablespoons lemon juice

3/4 cup arugula

1 garlic clove, peeled

1/2 cup olive oil

1/4 teaspoon lemon zest, grated

1 ½ pound uncooked shrimp, peeled and deveined

1/4 teaspoon salt

1/8 teaspoon ground black pepper

1/4 cup Parmesan cheese, shredded

Directions:

1. Take food processor or blender, open the lid and inside add the ingredients from the parsley to lemon zest.
2. Blend to make a smooth mixture. Add the salt, pepper, Parmesan cheese, and blend again.
3. Add the shrimps and combine them well. Refrigerate for 1 hour to marinate.
4. Take the skewers, thread the shrimps. Thread alternatively.
5. Take Ninja Foodi Grill, arrange it over your kitchen platform, and open the top lid.
6. Arrange the grill grate and close the top lid.
7. Press "GRILL" and select the "MED" grill function. Adjust the timer to 6 minutes and then press "START/STOP." Ninja Foodi will start pre-heating.

8. Ninja Foodi is preheated and ready to cook when it starts to beep. After you hear a beep, open the top lid.
9. Arrange the skewers over the grill grate.
10. Close the top lid and cook for 3 minutes. Now open the top lid, flip the skewers.
11. Close the top lid and cook for 3 more minutes.
12. Serve warm.

Nutritional Values (Per Serving):

Calories: 302
Fat: 16g
Saturated Fat: 2g
Trans Fat: 0g
Carbohydrates: 6g
Fiber: 1.5g
Sodium: 401mg
Protein: 33.5g

Crisped Fish Nuggets

Prep Time: 5-10 min.

Cooking Time: 20 min.

Number of Servings: 3-4

Ingredients:

½ cup all-purpose flour

1 tablespoon parmesan cheese

2 tablespoons coconut oil

2 cloves of garlic, chopped

3 white fish fillets, cut into cubes

Directions:

1. In a mixing bowl, mix the combine all the ingredients except the fish. Add the fillets and combine them well.
2. Refrigerate for 1-2 hours to marinate.
3. Take Ninja Foodi Grill, arrange it over your kitchen platform, and open the top lid.
4. Arrange the Crisping Basket inside the pot.
5. Press "AIR CRISP" and adjust the temperature to 390°F. Adjust the timer to 20 minutes and then press "START/STOP." Ninja Foodi will start pre-heating.
6. Ninja Foodi is preheated and ready to cook when it starts to beep. After you hear a beep, open the top lid.
7. Arrange the fish fillets directly inside the basket.
8. Close the top lid and allow to cook until the timer reads zero.
9. Serve warm.

Nutritional Values (Per Serving):

Calories: 203
Fat: 14.5g
Saturated Fat: 5g
Trans Fat: 0g
Carbohydrates: 9g
Fiber: 2g
Sodium: 286mg
Protein: 11g

Garlic Roasted Salmon

Prep Time: 5-10 min.

Cooking Time: 8 min.

Number of Servings: 4

Ingredients:

1 tablespoon olive oil

1 teaspoon dried basil

1 pound salmon fillet

2 cloves of garlic, minced

1 teaspoon ground black pepper

1/2 teaspoon salt

1 tablespoon parsley, chopped

1 tablespoon lemon juice

Directions:

1. In a mixing bowl, add all the ingredients except the salmon. Combine the ingredients to mix well with each other.
2. Add the salmon fillets and combine them well. Refrigerate for 1 hour to marinate.
3. Take Ninja Foodi Grill, arrange it over your kitchen platform, and open the top lid. Lightly grease cooking pot with some oil or cooking spray.
4. Press "ROAST" and adjust the temperature to 400°F. Adjust the timer to 8 minutes and then press "START/STOP." Ninja Foodi will start pre-heating.
5. Arrange the salmon fillets over the grill grate. Drizzle 1 tablespoon olive oil on top and add the leftover marinade on top.
6. Close the top lid and allow to cook until the timer reads zero.
7. Serve warm.

Nutritional Values (Per Serving):

Calories: 411
Fat: 21g
Saturated Fat: 4g
Trans Fat: 0g
Carbohydrates: 5g
Fiber: 1g
Sodium: 624mg
Protein: 45g

Grilled Soy Cod

Prep Time: 5-10 min.

Cooking Time: 15 min.

Number of Servings: 4

Ingredients:

3 tablespoons brown sugar

1 teaspoon sesame oil

1 pound baby bok choy, halved lengthwise

2 tablespoons soy sauce

1 tablespoon white wine or mirin

4 (6-ounce) cod fillets

¼ cup miso paste

¼ teaspoon red pepper flakes

Directions:

1. Take a zip-lock bag, add the cod, miso, brown sugar, ¾ teaspoon of sesame oil, and white wine.
2. Add the fillets and shake well. Refrigerate for 30 minutes.
3. Take Ninja Foodi Grill, arrange it over your kitchen platform, and open the top lid.
4. Arrange the grill grate and close the top lid.
5. Press "GRILL" and select the "MAX" grill function. Adjust the timer to 8 minutes and then press "START/STOP." Ninja Foodi will start pre-heating.
6. Ninja Foodi is preheated and ready to cook when it starts to beep. After you hear a beep, open the top lid.
7. Arrange the fillets over the grill grate.
8. Close the top lid and allow to cook until the timer reads zero.
9. Set aside the cooked fillets.
10. Press "GRILL" and select the "MAX" grill function. Adjust the timer to 9 minutes and then press "START/STOP." Ninja Foodi will start pre-heating.
11. Ninja Foodi is preheated and ready to cook when it starts to beep. After you hear a beep, open the top lid.
12. Arrange the bok choy over the grill grate.

13. Close the top lid and allow to cook until the timer reads zero.
14. Serve the grilled fish with the bok choy.

Nutritional Values (Per Serving):

Calories: 231
Fat: 4 g
Saturated Fat: 0.5g
Trans Fat: 0g
Carbohydrates: 15g
Fiber: 2g
Sodium: 1142mg
Protein: 33g

Mustard Green Veggies

Prep Time: 5-10 min.

Cooking Time: 30-40 min.

Number of Servings: 7-8

Ingredients:

Vinaigrette:

2 tablespoon Dijon mustard

1/2 cup red wine vinegar

2 tablespoon honey

1 teaspoon salt

1/4 teaspoon black pepper

1/2 cup avocado oil

1/2 cup olive oil

Veggies:

4 zucchinis, halved

4 sweet onions, quartered

4 red peppers, seeded and halved

2 bunches green onions, trimmed

4 yellow squash, cut in half

Directions:

1. In a small bowl, whisk the vinegar, mustard, honey, pepper, and salt. Add the oils and combine them to make a smooth mixture.

2. Take Ninja Foodi Grill, arrange it over your kitchen platform, and open the top lid.
3. Arrange the grill grate and close the top lid.
4. Press "GRILL" and select the "MED" grill function. Adjust the timer to 10 minutes and then press "START/STOP." Ninja Foodi will start pre-heating.
5. Ninja Foodi is preheated and ready to cook when it starts to beep. After you hear a beep, open the top lid.
6. Arrange the onion quarters over the grill grate.
7. Close the top lid and cook for 5 minutes. Now open the top lid, flip the onions.
8. Close the top lid and cook for 5 more minutes.
9. Grill the other vegetables in the same manner with 7 minutes per side for the zucchini, peppers, and squash. And 1 minute per side for the green onions.
10. Serve the grilled veggies with the vinaigrette on top.

Nutritional Values (Per Serving):

Calories: 326

Fat: 4.5g

Saturated Fat: 0.5g

Trans Fat: 0g

Carbohydrates: 35.5g

Fiber: 2g

Sodium: 524mg

Protein: 8g

Creamy Corn Potatoes

Prep Time: 5-10 min.

Cooking Time: 30-40 min.

Number of Servings: 4

Ingredients:

1 1/2 pound red potatoes, quartered and boiled

3 tablespoons olive oil

1 tablespoon cilantro, minced

2 sweet corn ears, without husks

1/4 teaspoon cayenne pepper

2 poblano peppers

1/2 cup milk

1 teaspoon ground cumin

1 tablespoon lime juice

1 jalapeno pepper, seeded and minced

1/2 cup sour cream

1 ½ teaspoons garlic salt

Directions:

1. Drain the potatoes and rub them with oil.
2. Take Ninja Foodi Grill, arrange it over your kitchen platform, and open the top lid.
3. Arrange the grill grate and close the top lid.
4. Press "GRILL" and select the "MED" grill function. Adjust the timer to 10 minutes and then press "START/STOP." Ninja Foodi will start pre-heating.
5. Ninja Foodi is preheated and ready to cook when it starts to beep. After you hear a beep, open the top lid.
6. Arrange the poblano peppers over the grill grate.
7. Close the top lid and cook for 5 minutes. Now open the top lid, flip the peppers.

8. Close the top lid and cook for 5 more minutes.
9. Grill the other vegetables in the same manner with 7 minutes per side for the potatoes and corn.
10. Whisk the remaining ingredients in another bowl.
11. Peel the grilled pepper and chop them. Divide corn ears into smaller pieces and cut the potatoes as well.
12. Serve the grilled veggies with the vinaigrette on top.

Nutritional Values (Per Serving):

Calories: 322
Fat: 4.5g
Saturated Fat: 1g
Trans Fat: 0g
Carbohydrates: 51.5g
Fiber: 3g
Sodium: 600mg
Protein: 5g

Vegetable Pasta Delight

Prep Time: 5-10 min.

Cooking Time: 15 min.

Number of Servings: 2-3

Ingredients:

1 small zucchini, sliced

1 small sweet yellow, halved

2/3 cups orzo pasta, cooked and drained

¼ pound fresh asparagus, trimmed

1 small portobello mushroom, stem removed

1/2 small red onion, halved

Salad dressing:

2 tablespoons balsamic vinegar

1 ½ tablespoons lemon juice

2 garlic cloves, minced

1 tablespoon olive oil

½ teaspoon lemon-pepper seasoning

Salad:

½ tablespoon minced parsley

½ tablespoon minced basil

1/4 teaspoon salt

½ cup grape tomatoes, halved

1/8 teaspoon pepper

½ cup (2 ounces) feta cheese, crumbled

Directions:

1. In two separate bowls, combine all the salad and dressing ingredients.
2. Take Ninja Foodi Grill, arrange it over your kitchen platform, and open the top lid.
3. Arrange the grill grate and close the top lid.
4. Press "GRILL" and select the "MED" grill function. Adjust the timer to 10 minutes and then press "START/STOP." Ninja Foodi will start pre-heating.
5. Ninja Foodi is preheated and ready to cook when it starts to beep. After you hear a beep, open the top lid.
6. Arrange the mushrooms, pepper, and onion over the grill grate.
7. Close the top lid and cook for 5 minutes. Now open the top lid, flip the vegetables.
8. Close the top lid and cook for 5 more minutes.
9. Grill the other vegetables in the same manner with 2 minutes per side for the zucchini and asparagus.
10. Dice the grilled vegetables; add them to the salad bowl. Add the pasta and top with the dressing; toss and serve.

Nutritional Values (Per Serving):

Calories: 234

Fat: 14g

Saturated Fat: 1g

Trans Fat: 0g

Carbohydrates: 38g

Fiber: 4g

Sodium: 369mg

Protein: 12g

Apple Green Salad

Prep Time: 5-10 min.

Cooking Time: 6 min.

Number of Servings: 2-3

Ingredients:

1/4 teaspoon Sriracha chili sauce

2 tablespoons cilantro, chopped

1/4 cup blue cheese, crumbled

1 apple, wedged

2 tablespoons orange juice

3 tablespoons avocado oil

1 tablespoon honey

1/4 teaspoon salt

2 tablespoons vinegar

½ garlic clove, minced

5 ounces salad greens

Directions:

1. In a mixing bowl, whisk the chili sauce, orange juice, oil, honey, vinegar, cilantro, garlic, and salt. Add 1/4th on the dressing with the apples in another bowl; toss well.
2. Take Ninja Foodi Grill, arrange it over your kitchen platform, and open the top lid.
3. Arrange the grill grate and close the top lid.
4. Press "GRILL" and select the "MED" grill function. Adjust the timer to 6 minutes and then press "START/STOP." Ninja Foodi will start pre-heating.
5. Ninja Foodi is preheated and ready to cook when it starts to beep. After you hear a beep, open the top lid.
6. Arrange the apples over the grill grate.
7. Close the top lid and cook for 3 minutes. Now open the top lid, flip the apples.

8. Close the top lid and cook for 3 more minutes.
9. Combine other ingredients in another bowl. Add the apples and top with the remaining dressing.
10. Serve warm.

Nutritional Values (Per Serving):

Calories: 406

Fat: 5g

Saturated Fat: 1.5g

Trans Fat: 0g

Carbohydrates: 48g

Fiber: 3g

Sodium: 517mg

Protein: 2g

Grilled Pineapple with Ice Cream

Prep Time: 5-10 min.

Cooking Time: 15 min.

Number of Servings: 5-6

Ingredients:

1/2 cup rum

1 pineapple, cored and sliced

1/2 cup packed brown sugar

1 teaspoon ground cinnamon

Vanilla ice cream to serve

Directions:

1. In a mixing bowl, mix run with cinnamon and brown sugar. Pour this mixture over the pineapple rings and coat evenly; set aside for 15 minutes.
2. Take Ninja Foodi Grill, arrange it over your kitchen platform, and open the top lid.
3. Arrange the grill grate and close the top lid.
4. Press "GRILL" and select the "MED" grill function. Adjust the timer to 8 minutes and then press "START/STOP." Ninja Foodi will start pre-heating.
5. Ninja Foodi is preheated and ready to cook when it starts to beep. After you hear a beep, open the top lid.
6. Arrange the pineapple slices over the grill grate.
7. Close the top lid and cook for 4 minutes. Now open the top lid, flip the slices.
8. Close the top lid and cook for 4 more minutes.
9. Serve warm with the ice cream scoop.

Nutritional Values (Per Serving):

Calories: 403
Fat: 29.5g
Saturated Fat: 4g
Trans Fat: 0g
Carbohydrates: 48.5g
Fiber: 13g
Sodium: 89mg
Protein: 11g

Choco Pecan Fudge

Prep Time: 5-10 min.

Cooking Time: 35 min.

Number of Servings: 10-12

Ingredients:

½ cup cocoa powder

4 eggs, beaten

2 cups white sugar

½ cup all-purpose flour

2 teaspoons vanilla extract

1 cup pecans, chopped

1 cup butter, melted

Directions:

1. In a mixing bowl, sift together the sugar, flour, and cocoa. Add the eggs, butter, vanilla, and pecans. Combine everything well.
2. Take a multi-purpose pan and lightly grease it with some cooking oil. In the pan, add the prepared batter.
3. Take Ninja Foodi Grill, arrange it over your kitchen platform, and open the top lid.
4. Press "BAKE" and adjust the temperature to 350°F. Adjust the timer to 35 minutes and then press "START/STOP." Ninja Foodi will start pre-heating.
5. Ninja Foodi is preheated and ready to cook when it starts to beep. After you hear a beep, open the top lid.
6. Arrange the pan directly inside the pot.
7. Close the top lid and allow to cook until the timer reads zero.
8. Serve warm.

Nutritional Values (Per Serving):

Calories: 361
Fat: 23.5g
Saturated Fat: 10g
Trans Fat: 0g
Carbohydrates: 39g
Fiber: 3g
Sodium: 91mg
Protein: 4g

Gorgeous Grilled Peaches

Prep Time: 5-10 min.

Cooking Time: 2 min.

Number of Servings: 4

Ingredients:

1/4 teaspoon cinnamon

4 ripe peaches, halved and pitted

1/4 cup salted butter

1 tablespoon + 1 teaspoon granulated sugar

Vegetable oil of your choice

Directions:

1. In a mixing bowl, combine the sugar with butter and cinnamon until the sugar dissolves.
2. Take Ninja Foodi Grill, arrange it over your kitchen platform, and open the top lid.
3. Arrange the grill grate and close the top lid.
4. Press "GRILL" and select the "MED" grill function. Adjust the timer to 2 minutes and then press "START/STOP." Ninja Foodi will start pre-heating.
5. Ninja Foodi is preheated and ready to cook when it starts to beep. After you hear a beep, open the top lid.
6. Arrange the peaches over the grill grate.
7. Close the top lid and cook for 1 minute. Now open the top lid, flip the peaches.
8. Close the top lid and cook for 1 more minute.
9. Serve the peaches with the butter on top.

Nutritional Values (Per Serving):

Calories: 392
Fat: 9g
Saturated Fat: 4g
Trans Fat: 0g
Carbohydrates: 51.5g
Fiber: 1.5g
Sodium: 287mg
Protein: 5g

Conclusion

Thanks again for taking your valuable time to read this book!

Just like millions of people, I, too, share the passion of devouring grilled cuisines. I throw parties, and outdoor get-to-gather, and grilled recipes have always been the center of attraction. My guests have always loved them and frankly speaking, who doesn't?

I wrote this book to provide an insight into this revolutionary Ninja Food Grill that blew my mind away with its ease of use and the ability to provide me with perfectly char-grilled recipes. Many people find it difficult to get the information they want about this unit, and that is why I wanted to include key information so that all the readers can get familiarize with various functions and features about this indoor grilling marvel.

This book aims at providing all readers a wide-range of versatile recipes to prepare for indoor grilling and savor them without worrying about enormous smoke and managing micro details of outdoor grilling units.

Have a great day! Eat healthy, live healthy!

Made in the USA
Monee, IL
17 November 2019